SRA OPEN COURT READING

Old Gold

A Division of The McGraw·Hill Companies

Columbus, Ohio

www.sra4kids.com

SRA/McGraw-Hill

A Division of The McGraw·Hill Companies

Send all inquiries to:
SRA/McGraw-Hill
8787 Orion Place
Columbus, OH 43240-4027

ISBN 0-07-569727-0
1 2 3 4 5 6 7 8 9 DBH 05 04 03 02 01

"See this map? I saw it in an old chest."

"You can hold it.
Go ahead and unfold it."

"The map tells us
where to find old gold."

"The gold is in the backyard.
The map told me so."

"The gold is over here by the fence.
Don't be scared, Tim. Be bold!"

"But, Mom, Oma got a map from an old chest. It has a mark for old gold."